A TUNE A DAY

For Classical Guitar
Repertoire Book 1
S. George Urwin

Contents

MUSIC FOR TWO GUITARS

Exclusively Distributed By

HAL•LEONARD®
CORPORATION

7777 W. BLUEMOUND RD. P.O. BOX 13819 MILWAUKEE, WI 53213

A TUNE A DAY

For Classical Guitar
Repertoire Book 1
S. George Urwin

Although this book is designed to supplement the material used in the Classical Guitar Books I and II from the Tune A Day Series, it may be readily incorporated into any similarly graded course of study, or used quite independently.

The pieces have been carefully selected to provide both a stimulus and a challenge, and to encourage musical and technical progress.

The duet section affords a valuable opportunity for early ensemble playing.

LITTLE WALTZ

F. CARULLI

DANCE

S. G. URWIN

PRELUDE

M. CARCASSI

B.M.Co. 13894

LULLABY

S. G. URWIN

MODERATO in A MINOR

F. CARULLI

B.M.Co. 13894

WALTZ in G

F. CARULLI

B.M.Co. 13894

WALTZ in A MINOR

M. CARCASSI

ANDANTINO in C

M. CARCASSI

STUDY I in A MINOR

D. AGUADO

TYROLEAN WALTZ

S. G. URWIN

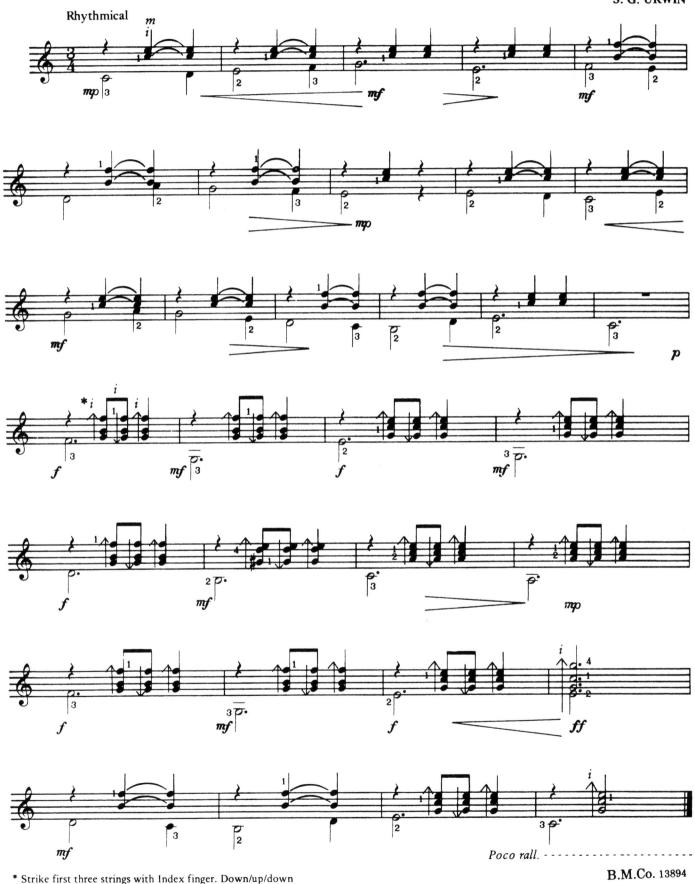

* Strike first three strings with Index finger. Down/up/down

B.M.Co. 13894

LÄNDLER

J. KÜFFNER

B.M.Co. 13894

RIVER SONG

S. G. URWIN

STUDY II in A MINOR

D. AGUADO

B.M.Co. 13894

* Alternative simpler fingering for this bar.

ALLEGRETTO in C

F. SOR

B.M.Co. 13894

LÄNDLER

A. DIABELLI

There are two points to watch in this piece.

(1) In Bar I the first G must be played on the 4th string. Likewise in line four following the double bar, the first E must be played on the 2nd string.

(2) The groups of notes marked 3 are triplets. This means that three equal notes must be played to each beat.

* *sf* − *sforzando* = Play with a strong accent.

SONATINA

F. CARULLI

Moderato

B.M.Co. 13894

B.M.Co. 13894

ANDANTE

A. DIABELLI

Poco rall.

MUSIC FOR TWO GUITARS

GREENSLEEVES

*Chords: A Min.

G   E Min.

A Min.   E Min.   A Min.   G   E Min.

A Min.   E   A Min.   C   G   E Min.   A Min.

E Min.   C   G   E Min.   A Min.   E   A Min.

B.M.Co. 13894

* An alternative, or additional accompaniment can be provided by playing the chords indicated.

PLAISIR D'AMOUR

G. MARTINI

TEMPO DI MARCIA

J. KÜFFNER

Guitar I

Guitar II

Fine

Da Capo al Fine

WALTZ

J. KÜFFNER

Guitar I

Guitar II

Fine

Da Capo al fine

**Simpler version for those unable to manage the F chord – I

II

B.M.Co. 13894